JOHN ROMERIL was born in Melbourne in 1945 and while a Monash University undergraduate wrote his first plays, the most noteworthy being *I Don't Know Who to Feel Sorry For* (1969) and *Chicago, Chicago* (1969–70). Romeril helped found the Australian Performing Group in 1970, and until it wound-up in 1981 the first performances of his plays were usually at the Pram Factory. Examples include *Mrs Thally F*, *Bastardy*, *The Floating World*, *The Golden Holden*, *Mickey's Moomba* and *Carboni*. He co-wrote APG successes like *Marvellous Melbourne*, *The Hills Family Show*, *Dudders* and *Waltzing Matilda*; and collaborated on most of the APG's outdoor, factory and touring shows.

In 1974 Romeril wrote the screenplay for *The Great McCarthy*, and his occasional film and television writing includes a twelve-part series for the ABC's education unit, *Six of the Best* (1982); and, with Rachel Perkins, *One Night The Moon* (2000).

Romeril's produced plays, premiered by various managements during the 1980s include *Samizdat*, *Definitely the Last*, *Jonah*, *The Kelly Dance*, *Legends*, *Lost Weekend*, *Top End* and *Koori Radio*, and he helped shape Manning Clark's *History of Australia: The Musical*. Produced plays from the 1990s include: *Black Cargo*, *Bring Down the House*, *Reading Boy*, *Doing the Block*, *Expo: The Human Factor*, *Acronetic*, *Kate 'n' Shiner*, *Love Suicides* and *Hanoi-Melbourne*.

Romeril's most recent produced major play was for Playbox, *Miss Tanaka* (2001). Since then he has concentrated on dramaturgical work, often with young writers; on research-driven community projects such as *Landmines*, *The Dukes of Windsor* and *Dancing The Line*, which await production; and on his role as Honorary Chair of Strange Fruit (since 2006), a Melbourne-based largely outdoor physical performance group whose work on sway poles has toured the world.

He has been Playwright-in-Residence with certain theatre companies and tertiary institutions thanks to support from the Literature Board of the Australia Council, and educational, civic and sometimes philanthropic entities. Prizes include the Canada-Australia Literary Award (1976) and the Patrick White Award (2008).

Miss Tanaka

John Romeril
adapted from a story by **Xavier Herbert**

CURRENCY PRESS
SYDNEY

CURRENCY PLAYS

First published in 2001
by Currency Press Pty Ltd,
PO Box 2287, Strawberry Hills, NSW, 2012, Australia
enquiries@currency.com.au
www.currency.com.au

in association with Playbox Theatre, Melbourne

Reprinted 2002, 2013.

NATIONAL LIBRARY OF AUSTRALIA CIP DATA

Romeril, John, 1945–.
  Miss Tanaka.
  ISBN 9780868196398.
  1. Pearl industry and trade—Australia—Drama. I. Herbert, Xavier, 1901–1984.
  II. Playbox Theatre (Melbourne, Vic.). III. Title. (Series: Current theatre series).
  A822.3

Typeset by Erin Dewar for Currency Press.
Cover design by Katy Wall for Currency Press.
Currency Press acknowledges the Traditional Owners of the Country on which we live and work. We pay our respects to all Aboriginal and Torres Strait Islander Elders, past and present.

Contents

For Noriko Nishimoto, who first ran with the idea.

Miss Tanaka was first produced by Handspan Visual Theatre and Playbox Theatre at The C.U.B. Malthouse, Melbourne, on 21 February 2001 with the following cast:

KAZUHIKO	Bradley Byquar
MR TANAKA	Tam Phan
MOTT	Jeremy Stanford
HANIF	Tony Yap
SAKAMOTO	Yumi Umiumare
PUPPETEERS	Megan Cameron
	Heather Monk
MUSICIANS	Junko Sakamoto
	Toshi Sakamoto

Director/Script Collaborator, David Bell
Composer, Darrin Verhagen
Set & Costume Designer, Greg Clarke
Lighting Designer, David Walters
Puppet Designer, Rob Matson
Puppetry Director, Heather Monk
Choreographer, Andris Toppe
Dramaturg, Louise Gough

CHARACTERS

KAZUHIKO, a young man of mixed Aboriginal and Japanese descent

TANAKA SENIOR, his Japanese father, an ex-diver now partly crippled

CHARLES MOTT, a young Englishman of Jewish extraction, new head of the Anglo-Oriental Pearlshell Company

HANIF MOHAMMED PUTU RODRIGUES DA COSTA, a diver of Malay heritage

SAKAMOTO FUJI, a Japanese diver

MISS KITSO, the Miss Tanaka of the title, is doubled by the actor performing Kazuhiko

TWO PUPPETEERS, double as crew members, sumo wrestlers, etc.

TWO MUSICIANS, frame but occasionally enter the action, and of course supply live accompaniment

THE FACE OF AN ABORIGINAL WOMAN, Kazuhiko's dead mother is sometimes projected

SETTING

Broome in late 1939.

The stage apron, two puppeteers perform a tiny puppet play, like a ritual, concerning water and a pearl.

SCENE ONE: BEACH, BROOME, A BEGINNING

To the sound of drumming, the black curtain opens.

We see a young Aboriginal/Asian man in his early twenties. He is squatting on a rock in the centre of a white void looking out towards the audience. The rock is made of crumpled white paper.

Downstage, we see the reflection of the moon on the water. Slowly the reflection begins to swell and move towards him.

As the wave breaks on the rock, he takes a small paper boat and sets it adrift on the water. As he does, we hear the distant sound of women singing a traditional Japanese song. Then we see two kimono-clad figures cross at the rear tracing the steps of an obon dance.

SONG: tsuki ga-a
        detta de-ta
        tsuki ga-a
        detta
        a yoi yoi
        ni de tanko o-no
        ue ni-i detta-a-a
        am-ari
        ento tsu ga-a
        takai-i no de-e-e
        sa-a zoo yaa
        otsuki sa-n
        kemu ta-a
        karo ara
        yoi yoi

The man slowly stands as the wave gets higher and the boat begins to float out to sea. The ghostly geishas have gone.

There is the sound of a crashing wave. The boat disappears. We are now under the ocean. Everything moves slower.

A large luminous pearl comes out of the gloom. The man is transfixed and slowly follows it.

As it moves to one side of the stage, the white curtain upstage slowly begins to open. Behind it is a black void. In it floats a luminous black pearl.

At one point, the stage looks as if it has been sliced in half: a white pearl floating in a white space, a black pearl floating in black.

The white pearl disappears as the curtain opens fully.

The man turns upstage and sees the black pearl floating in the black void.

A huge close-up of a beautiful young Aboriginal woman is projected on the black gauze at the front of the void. We can still see the black pearl floating upstage behind the image.

Downstage, the rock begins to move. Maybe it's a turtle.

But the turtle stands. It is an old-looking, but really only middle-aged Japanese man, draped in the crumpled piece of 'rock' paper. On the screen, the young woman smiles. The old man slowly turns his head and looks back at the young man.

The young man turns away from the image of the woman and the pearl and looks at the old man.

The paper falls, revealing how the old man's back is covered with tattoos.

Suddenly a very large Japanese-style kite of a shark 'swims' fast through the void.

The young man turns back just in time to see it swallow the pearl. He cries out.

The shark disappears. The image of the woman disappears.

The sound builds.

Blackout.

SCENE TWO: NIGHT VISTOR

A wave crashes leaving the sound of music: a 1934 recording (by Anne Lerner with Carroll Gibbons and His Boyfriends) of 'Smoke Gets In Your Eyes'.

Upstage, another man enters, immaculate in a 1930s white planter's suit. We hear his thoughts over the music—he is English:

MOTT: [*voice-over*] I knew how, for six decades, the rich pearling grounds off North-Western Australia had supplied eighty percent of the world's mother of pearl. From my grandfather and father's stories I knew too what dangerous waters these were. That in Exmouth to the south, the tide's twice daily rise and fall averaged six metres, while in King Sound to the north, a bay the size of Hungary, the same tidal rise and fall was eleven metres or more. But little could have prepared me for how much rising and falling of my own I'd be doing during my first week in Broome.

> *He walks downstage to the water's edge and stares out to sea through a pair of binoculars.*

> *The Aboriginal man is sitting where we first saw him.*

> *Sound effects of a 1930s plane travelling overhead.* MOTT *lowers the binoculars to look up and read its passage. The music continues quite loud.*

> *Looking around, the young Englishman realises he's not alone. He indicates the plane—eyeing its progress away from them.*

MOTT: Just in. Caught the night mail plane up from Perth. There it goes—on to Wyndham. Darwin the stop after that. They say, as an organisation, it has a future—Qantas. [*Pause.*] Mind you, after the flight I'm not wholly convinced.

> *He smiles—but has his humour missed its mark? The young man seems oblivious to his presence.*

Charles—Charles Alconquin Rubin Mott.

Still no response. It's as if—despite the perceptible fading of the plane sound effect—the other man isn't hearing a word. MOTT *walks towards him saying:*

The Mott family? The Anglo-Oriental Pearlshell Company? Carnavon Street?

The music finishes with a huge scratch as if someone has knocked the stylus off the record. The young man has the look of someone pulled from a dream against his will.

You're?

KAZUHIKO: Kaz-u-hi-ko.

MOTT *is dumb-struck as if he has heard someone speak Martian.*

MOTT: No speaka da English?

KAZUHIKO: It's my name.

MOTT: A thousand pardons. But you're—?

KAZUHIKO: Japanese father.

MOTT: In from London, via New York, then Hong Kong. Had planned a stop in Tokyo—it didn't work out.

MOTT *smiles—a little embarrassed—then looks out to sea through his binoculars.* KAZUHIKO *observes him.*

KAZUHIKO: Watching for your boats to come in, Mr Mott?

MOTT: Yes.

KAZUHIKO: If the fleet comes in tonight—it'll come round the point.

Taking the hint MOTT *trains his binoculars in the direction suggested. Pause.*

Wondering if the company assets will make it back to port in ship-shape condition?

MOTT: That's more or less the picture.

KAZUHIKO: Loaded with treasure. [*Beat.*] Let's hope they don't sink—there's no insurance in the pearling game.

MOTT: So Lloyds keep telling me.

KAZUHIKO *smiles faintly.* MOTT *does not answer but keeps scanning the horizon. As he looks out to sea we hear* MOTT *with ocean sound effects under.*

MOTT: [*voice-over*] I toy with the idea of telling this newly-met fellow: yes, money—and lots of it—is uppermost in my mind. Admitting how, on the other side of the world, in Poland, Hungary, Czechoslovakia, let alone Germany itself, I have a brace of relatives whose lives can yet be saved, provided the cash is there. How they are indeed relying on me, and a good haul of pearlshell. But might not wearing my heart on my sleeve simply be to, as it were, cast pearls before swine? What would that mean here? Talk of Hitler— the thousand year Reich?

> *Back to reality.*

KAZUHIKO: Those lenses Czech?

MOTT: German.

KAZUHIKO: Better anyway than these.

> KAZUHIKO *has produced a pair of opera glasses from the folds of his shirt. They are decorated with mother of pearl.*

MOTT: Opera glasses?

KAZUHIKO: My father gave them to my mother when they were married.

MOTT: They're exquisite.

KAZUHIKO: Part of a set: the opera glasses, a cigarette case, and a fan. All inlaid mother of pearl.

MOTT: May I?

KAZUHIKO: [*handing them to* MOTT] Everything else my father pawned—those I've managed to hide and hang onto.

MOTT: Is there opera in Broome?

> MOTT *admires and raises the opera glasses to scan the horizon.*

KAZUHIKO: No, but there's kabuki in Osaka. He was always going to take her to see it.

MOTT: Was?

KAZUHIKO: Not all promises get kept.

MOTT: I have something similar from my mother. She pressed it on me. 'You can't be too careful, Charles—not in the tropics.'

> *He is producing a tiny revolver from his pocket. He hands it to* KAZUHIKO.

KAZUHIKO: Does it work?

MOTT: Never loaded as far as I know.

KAZUHIKO: Mother of pearl handle.

MOTT: Beautiful, isn't it?

KAZUHIKO: Not if you die getting the pearlshell.

KAZUHIKO will aim—then return the pistol.

MOTT: Your mother's from Broome?

KAZUHIKO: Thursday Island. Father won her in a card game.

MOTT: How—colourful.

KAZUHIKO: Then lost her, in King Sound. They're dangerous waters. She was working with him, trying to repair our family's fortunes. She's gone but the old goat remains. [*Pause.*] A legend round here, my father. Rated Broome's Number One Diver three seasons running—no mean feat when fifteen years is about as long as a diver gets.

MOTT: Are you a diver?

KAZUHIKO: After what happened to my mother? No thanks.

MOTT: Not following in your father's footsteps?

KAZUHIKO: When you see the way he walks you'll know why I avoid diving like the plague. Forty going on sixty-five—a man made old before his time. These days all he wants is to return home to die.

MOTT: To Japan?

KAZUHIKO: To Taiji. That's in Wakayama.

A voice nearby mumbles as if woken from a dream:

TANAKA: Taiji.

KAZUHIKO: God knows why he calls it home—he left there when he was five.

Again the voice:

TANAKA: The best divers always come from Taiji.

MOTT is mystified as to the source of this new voice. He turns only to see the rock move and an old man crawl quickly toward him. This is old MR TANAKA.

Mott! Mr Mott!

KAZUHIKO: Pay him no heed. He's a mental and physical wreck.

MOTT: A wreck? Seconds earlier I'd thought him a rock.

KAZUHIKO: Keep sleeping it off.

TANAKA: How about you pay my fare back to Taiji?

MOTT: What?

TANAKA: Pay my fare—back to Taiji.

MOTT: I hardly think that will be—

TANAKA: Taiji, Mr Mott!

MOTT: I'm not Mr Mott! Well I am, but [*to* MR TANAKA] my father is dead! I'm his son. I've recently become the new head of Anglo-Oriental.

A moment as the old man takes this in. MOTT *is uneasy.*

TANAKA: Ah.

MOTT: There's a family likeness.

KAZUHIKO: Between me and my father—thanks very much.

MOTT: No, between my father and me—could never see it myself but your father obviously picked up on it.

The old man is now crawling forward toward the sea as if searching for something.

TANAKA: I leased a lugger from old Mr Mott. Kept him in pearlshell for fifteen years.

KAZUHIKO *and* MOTT *watch* TANAKA SENIOR'*s progress.*

KAZUHIKO: The nitrogen in his blood's crippled him. Tortoru Sentoro— 'Old Turtle Back' they call him. Pathetic. People risking their sanity, their limbs, their lives—to what end? So we can boast buttons on our shirts, or in New York or Paris some sleek socialite can do up— or undo—a string of pearls.

There is a soft swell of music. MOTT *looks around.*

MOTT: The moon?

KAZUHIKO: Rising.

Interwoven is a woman's voice.

Puppeteers enter from one side rolling a large disk of wobbly mirror. During the sequence they reflect light from a specially-rigged spotlight and manipulate the disc so it reflects a trail of shimmering light over the set. The effect should be quite magical.

VOICE-OVER: Like a pearl
    A giant pearl
    The moon hanging over Broome
    Kisses the township and creeps
    Forward bathing the beach to finally reach
    The shore—there to leave
    On each wave
    A glitter, a shimmer, a glimmer, a flicker
    That soon is a ribbon, a river
    Of light
    A mystic stream
    You'd glimpse in a dream
    With an ebb a surge a flow
    It's as though
    A celestial arrow's been
    Shot at the black of the night!

> *The music continues under.* MOTT *is impressed by this unexpected phenomenon.*

KAZUHIKO: 'The Pearl Road'.

MOTT: You have a name for it?

KAZUHIKO: Two of them. From here we call it 'The Pearl Road'. For the pearlers out there, coming homewards, it's 'The Golden Stairway to the Moon'.

> *The music swells again.*

VOICE-OVER: As it travels unravels widens unwinds
    That avenue of light seems like
    A rainbow-ribboned seam
    Edging the black cloak of Night
    It's as if
    A million a billion a trillion pearlshell buttons
    Have been fixed, sewn, stitched to the hem
    Of the cape Night has thrown
    Across the ocean's swell—

MOTT: Well I never.

> *The moment is held, then:*

TANAKA: Lights!

There is a sudden change of mood. The sound swells—big music/ drumming etc. The puppeteers disappear.

SCENE THREE: NIGHT AND THE FLEET SAILS HOME.

KAZUHIKO *and* MOTT *hasten downstage and look out to sea through their respective opera glasses/binoculars. Urgent music under. The stage is filled with thousands of reflections of light bouncing off water.*

MOTT: The boats—they're so low in the water.

KAZUHIKO: Weighed down by the harvest.

TANAKA: It's a good haul.

MOTT: But none of it insured—what if they lose the lot?

TANAKA: That funny sailing all for show.

KAZUHIKO: Got the brains of chooks with their heads cut off.

MOTT: I own fifty-eight of those luggers, three of those mother schooners, that wood and water train we lease out to a third party— sink even a quarter of that shipping and the company sinks!

The old man has seen something new. He's excited.

TANAKA: Glasses!

MOTT *hands him the binoculars.*

MOTT: What's he seen?

KAZUHIKO *looks out to sea through the opera glasses.*

KAZUHIKO: That black smudge to the right.

MOTT: What about it?

KAZUHIKO: Could be a mini-cyclone—even a cockeyed bob.

MOTT: A cockeyed what?

The sound swells. And the old man talks louder over the growing soundscape.

TANAKA: Ha! Go, Taiji! They're getting hurled round Entrance Point like fleas stuck to a mad dog's tail!

Which calms MOTT *not a jot. The music and effects build. The old man unwinds the scarf from round his head to mop his face.*

Weather. They'll try and tell me this is weather.

SCENE FOUR: LANDFALL BY NIGHT

*The white curtain opens. The prows of two boats crash through opposing walls of the set. Each boat has huge and fierce images of their owners painted on them in bright colours like figureheads. A beat later, the boat owners (*HANIF *and* SAKAMOTO*) enter upstage, swinging in on ropes 'Tarzan-style' from opposite directions. They are dressed in brightly-coloured costumes which match their boats. They land and tumble onto the stage. They immediately start squabbling. In counterpoint, separate instruments underscore each man's utterance—a duet of anger.*

SAKAMOTO: You cut across my bows out there, little man!

HANIF: Which you think I did on purpose?

SAKAMOTO: No—but you did it!

HANIF: You know what the weather's like out there!

SAKAMOTO: And I know out there you cut across my bows!

> SAKAMOTO *pushes* HANIF *aside.* MOTT*'s hearing the music, not the words. All this is the babble of foreign tongues to him.*

HANIF: Sakamoto Fuji's pride has been wounded—maybe I should kiss it better—with my kris!

> *He produces a kris—*SAKAMOTO *reaches for and receives a gaff iron. They circle each other warily.* MOTT *looks on, decidedly apprehensive.*

SAKAMOTO: [*in Japanese*] Pork eater!

MOTT: [*to* KAZUHIKO] What are they saying?!

KAZUHIKO: [*to* MOTT] Pork eater!

HANIF: [*in Malay*] Rice muncher!

KAZUHIKO: [*to* MOTT] Rice muncher!

SAKAMOTO: [*in Japanese*] Pig licker!

KAZUHIKO: [*to* MOTT] Pig licker!

HANIF: [*in Malay*] Soy-bean fart machine!

KAZUHIKO: [*to* MOTT] Soy-bean fart machine!

MOTT: They certainly have a way with words.

> *They charge—miss each other—pull back to circle again.*

Again their utterance is in English, but it's like the instruments underscoring their words are at war.

SAKAMOTO: First boat back—but why? Little Hanif—little harvest.

HANIF: Big Sakamoto—big harvest—but why so big?

SAKAMOTO: Because I work harder, work longer—plenty more shell. Diver Number One.

HANIF: How much chicken shell in your sacks? Little oyster, baby one. Diver Number One? You Pirate Number One!

They fight a swashbuckling battle that combines both Malay and Japanese martial arts. KAZUHIKO *and* MOTT *are caught in the middle of the fracas. There's a brief lull.*

You Japanese plunder the sea! We Malays farm it.

SAKAMOTO: You Malays couldn't farm parsley in a bucket!

The fight resumes. Puppeteers are acting as crew members.

MOTT: This is—

KAZUHIKO: Broome, Mr Mott.

CREW: Go, Sakamoto Fuji-san!

The old man looks from the combatants to MOTT *and back, laughing like a maniac.*

Go, Hanif Mohammed Putu Rodrigues da Costa!

MOTT: Gentlemen, please. My card!

KAZUHIKO: It's not your card.

MOTT *realises he has pulled out the revolver and is holding it aloft. He pockets it and withdraws his business card offering it for their edification. The warring parties pause wondering what this interruption can mean.*

They're not big readers of English. Should I translate?

KAZUHIKO *takes* MOTT'*s card.*

[*Reading slowly*] Charles Alconquin Rubin Mott—The Anglo-Oriental Pearlshell Company. [*To* MOTT] Do you want me to give the address?

MOTT: I think they know the location.

KAZUHIKO: Buyers of pearlshell since 1898.

MOTT: Buyers of pearlshell. My grandfather—my father—now me.

A beat as MOTT *lets that sink in. That's the card done with—an appeal to reason has begun.*

I have from my father…

KAZUHIKO *starts to 'translate'* MOTT'*s speech. A mix of instruments start up, representing the various languages.*

And from my grandfather before him, something of this town's history. [*To* KAZUHIKO] How many languages are you using?

KAZUHIKO: Japanese and Malay—with Tagalog, Tetum and Bardi for the others.

MOTT: Will it be enough?

KAZUHIKO: I think everyone's getting the gist.

MOTT: 1907.

Silence. And a beat.

KAZUHIKO: You want me to translate that?

MOTT: Please.

KAZUHIKO: 1907.

MOTT: 1914.

KAZUHIKO: 1914.

MOTT: 1920.

KAZUHIKO: 1920.

MOTT: Do those years mean nothing to us?

The translation instruments see-saw away as KAZUHIKO *deals now with* SAKAMOTO *now with* HANIF *now with the crew members—and even the old man.* MOTT *paces—pausing appropriately—a latter-day Disraeli warming to the task of statesmanship.*

Wise men learn from history. Fools repeat it. A race riot is easy to start. Not so easy to end.

This has all taken some time. But at its end the fighting simply resumes.

What are they saying?

The instruments are going as SAKAMOTO *and* HANIF *yell and stamp and scowl and snort afresh. Like the calm centre of a storm,* KAZUHIKO *informs* MOTT *of what's what.*

KAZUHIKO: Sakamoto's saying: What about 1937 when those Koepanger bastards tried to lynch every Japanese bastard they could get their hands on!

MOTT: And the other chap?

KAZUHIKO: He's saying: A pity the cyclone of 1935 left so few of you Japanese bastards to find!

TANAKA: 1935—that was weather, Mr Mott, serious weather.

MOTT: They're not going to stop, are they?

> HANIF *and* SAKAMOTO *lunge and lock together in a sumo-style hold.*

KAZUHIKO: It's out again!

MOTT: What is? Aw my God!

> MOTT *realises he's again holding the revolver aloft. He'd repocket it but it's too late. This time everyone's seen it. They eye him and it warily. What will the white man do next is the question. A beat. He gestures limply.*

It's—it's a joke—it's a toy—it's—for emphasis—not even loaded, I'll show you—

> *Bang. But loaded it is. Everyone except* MOTT *and* KAZUHIKO *dives for cover.* MOTT *can't believe his bad luck.* KAZUHIKO *can't believe what a fool the man is, but smiles.*

KAZUHIKO: That's put the cat amongst the pigeons.

> HANIF *and* SAKAMOTO *are yelling in Malay and Japanese.*

MOTT: A mistake, a terrible mis— [*To* KAZUHIKO] What's being said?

KAZUHIKO: [*listening*] That's not a gun. This is a gun. [*He listens.*] This is a gun. This is a gun. This is a gun. And this is: a kris.

> *Everyone pulls out an increasingly bigger gun (capped by* HANIF*'s kris) and point them* MOTT *and* KAZUHIKO*'s way.* KAZUHIKO *starts addressing the divers again in various languages and the instruments clash and clang away.*

MOTT: What are you telling them?

KAZUHIKO: That you're an idiot.

MOTT *opens his mouth to speak but thinks better of it when he hears the sound of guns being cocked.*

And they should forgive you.

More talking from KAZUHIKO. HANIF *and* SAKAMOTO *talk back and over the top of him. Every so often they all stop and peer at* MOTT, *then continue their instrument-inflected discussion. Finally* KAZUHIKO *crosses back to* MOTT *to update him on developments.*

I've told them that you're new to Broome. That it'll take you a while to learn the ropes. You won't always know the real import of what you see. For example—

MOTT: For example what?

KAZUHIKO: I told them how you thought they were lairising out on the bay when really it was the weather and they were all sailing for dear life.

MOTT: I did—I did think that [*to* HANIF *and* KAZUHIKO] and I'm very sorry.

The divers and crews relax a little.

KAZUHIKO: But you had Anglo-Oriental's fleet to worry about—and the harvest.

MOTT: That's right.

KAZUHIKO: Above all, seeing Hanif and Sakamoto at each other's throats, you misread the situation, feared a race riot might develop, and made an utter dill of yourself.

MOTT: I did, didn't I?

TANAKA: Did you ever!

MOTT *opens his mouth to excuse himself further—but the divers are advancing. He stiffens fearing the worst.*

SAKAMOTO: Did Mr Mott really think I wanted to snuff Hanif Mohammed Putu Rodrigues da Costa out like a candle? Ha ha ha!

He whacks old man TANAKA *on the back.*

HANIF: Did he really think I wanted to rip Sakamoto Fuji's heart from its hole? Ha ha ha!

And he whacks the old man on the back. They form a trio of divers. Pals in the diving fraternity.

KAZUHIKO: Broome, Mr Mott—where men are men—

MOTT: And I have a lot to learn.

The crew members fire off a fusillade of shots into the air causing MOTT *to drop to the ground. Laughing at this* HANIF, SAKAMOTO *and the puppeteers leave.*

TANAKA: They like you, they really like you.

They've gone. MOTT *looks at the debris.*

MOTT: They leave the boats like that? All higgledy-piggledy?

KAZUHIKO: The bright lights of Broome beckon.

TANAKA: Four months at sea—

The old man is staring off the way the divers have gone.

MOTT: But the harvest. No one's guarding it.

TANAKA: Tell him.

KAZUHIKO: Broome's last known pearlshell thief was found in Dampier Creek—a tomahawk cleaving his skull, a severed testicle swelling each cheek.

MOTT: You're not joining the others?

KAZUHIKO: First night of the lay-up? The circus came to Broome once—and it was better.

A black gauze is pulled across the scene behind them as we cross-fade to these three on the beach.

Squatting, KAZUHIKO *takes a piece of paper from inside his shirt and starts folding it origami-style.* MOTT *lingers, looking from* KAZUHIKO *to the old man and back. Then he divines what* KAZUHIKO *is up to:*

MOTT: It's a boat!

KAZUHIKO: You have a fleet—I have this.

TANAKA: And if it's August 15, I'm Mount Fuji!

MOTT: What's he mean—August 15?

KAZUHIKO: Obon Odori and—

TANAKA: The Toto Nagashi!

KAZUHIKO *goes back to his boat.* MOTT *comes closer. The old man has gone into a dance position.*

KAZUHIKO: We hold a Festival for Lost Souls.

Soft musical underscore—incorporating snatches of the song from Scene One—has begun and the old man starts to dance. It's a sake-addled ruse to exit and follow the divers, but he fears KAZUHIKO *will try to detain him.*

On that night the whole Japanese community gathers. The ladies of Sheba Lane, in their geisha finery, lead the ceremonial song and dance, the steps of which the bumble-footed one is showing you. A pale blue lantern is lit and placed on every Japanese grave in the cemetery. A larger lantern still is put on the grave of whichever diver or crew member has most recently met their end.

The old man has danced further and further away.

[*Shouting to his father*] Where are you off to?

TANAKA: Home—to bed!

KAZUHIKO: Liar! For days we prepare miniature boats. Load them with rice, fish, fruit, sake, supplies for the journey, each festooned with flowers, each bearing a tiny lantern to guide the way, at midnight we launch them—from here.

MOTT: Every August 15?

TANAKA: Only he does it any old month, day or night.

KAZUHIKO: Some are content to recall the dead one day of the year—

MOTT: You do so more often?

KAZUHIKO: It's to make the passage from this world to the next a successful crossing for our dear but departed ancestral spirits.

The old man has gone but the song continues.

MOTT: Your mother—she's the dear and departed ancestral spirit you're making that for?

KAZUHIKO: Aren't you a deep reader of the human comedy?

Pause. MOTT *is unsure how to take this last statement.*

There is distant shouting and laughter from offstage. Maybe some more rifle fire. MOTT *looks towards the noise.*

MOTT *turns back to* KAZUHIKO *then decides to go off towards town.*

MOTT: Goodnight then.

He starts to exit.

KAZUHIKO: I'd keep that pistol in my pocket if I were you.

KAZUHIKO *is alone. In the far rear distance a small hill is dotted with tiny blue lights—Broome's Japanese graveyard. The song rises in volume and swirls into the next scene.*

SCENE FIVE: THE NIGHTLIFE OF BROOME

Film sequence. The sequence is a combination of screen images projected on the front gauze, and stage images softly lit behind.

Establishing shots of Broome township, jetty, boats, divers, finally a street.

Cut to HANIF *and* SAKAMOTO *in the street. Before they were at each other's throats, now they exchange a big hug.*

SAKAMOTO: Tomodachi!
HANIF: Kawan!
SAKAMOTO: Kawan!
HANIF: Tomodachi!

They disappear into a doorway.

TANAKA SENIOR *hurries in. He pauses looking for the others.*

We hear music played loudly on a scratchy gramophone mixed with the sounds of men drinking, talking and shouting.

Someone gets thrown out of a doorway in front of MR TANAKA. *A bouncer has ejected a punter from a brothel.*

MR TANAKA *looks in that doorway.*

Brothel. Interior. HANIF *and* SAKAMOTO *are each with a prostitute. The group sees* MR TANAKA *and laughs.*

SAKAMOTO: Here to write love's story with your pencil stub, Saichi Tanaka-san?

TANAKA: Just seeing what you're up to.
HANIF: First the cockfight, old man—then the cockfight!

Everyone laughs.

TANAKA: I'll see you there.

Suddenly the old guy too is getting thrown into the street. As he picks himself up MOTT *enters.* TANAKA SENIOR *collars him.*

You won't buy an old diver a ticket to Taiji—but how about a drink?

MOTT *considers the idea.*

Or something.
MOTT: Or something?

Opium den. On screen: MR TANAKA *smoking opium.* MOTT *is with him looking decidedly mellow. The room swims.*

A cockfight. On screen: a noisy crowd.

On stage we see the puppeteers, their arms wrapped in paper so that they appear to be holding cockerels. They are dancing a tango as they perform a cockfight, their hands act as the heads/ beaks. As they dance they fight. MOTT *is seen watching all this with the look of a tourist on the 'Nightlife of Broome' tour. He is joined by* HANIF *and* SAKAMOTO.

On screen: close-up of HANIF, SAKAMOTO *and other punters yelling and shouting.*

On stage: the fight builds and the puppeteers peck and tear each other's puppet cockerel to pieces.

Screen: a whirlwind of feathers fills the screen.

When it clears we see MOTT *seated on stage with* HANIF, SAKAMOTO *and* TANAKA SENIOR *playing mahjong.*

When it finishes the old man loses but proceeds to pour the others sake in a delicate etiquette-respecting manner.

TANAKA: I pour for Mr Mott.
SAKAMOTO: Our guest.

TANAKA: I pour for you, Sakamoto Fuji-san. And I pour for you, Hanif Mohammed Putu Rodrigues da Costa.

SAKAMOTO: And pour for yourself.

TANAKA: I am unworthy. But thank you—I will. Kampai!

As the others sip appreciatively, the old guy glugs from the bottle. We're in a gambling den.

On screen: a roulette wheel spinning.

On stage: MOTT *is looking around, bemused.*

MOTT: The Resident Magistrate's official residence, eh?

HANIF: Open all hours.

TANAKA: For gambling.

HANIF *and* SAKAMOTO *put some money down before* MR TANAKA. *He picks it up respectfully and explains.*

Young divers look after old divers.

MOTT: So I see.

MR TANAKA *sees on the screen the huge close-ups of* HANIF *and* SAKAMOTO *looking down at him.*

SAKAMOTO: When that's gone, you're gone.

HANIF: Not running the Saichi Tanaka Old Diver's Charity Fund, you know.

Screen: noisy crowd in the gambling den. MR TANAKA *in a card game with* HANIF.

On stage: a large monkey appears. It reminds us of HANIF. MR TANAKA, *sitting upstage centre in the black void, plays cards with this monkey. It wins and is jubilant.*

On screen: HANIF *jubilant.*

Screen: a giant roulette wheel spins and MOTT *now very drunk tries to read its whirl.*

Screen: MR TANAKA *plays cards with* SAKAMOTO.

On stage: a large frog appears. It reminds us of SAKAMOTO. MR TANAKA *plays cards with it. It wins and is jubilant.*

On screen: SAKAMOTO *jubilant. The roulette wheel spins.* MOTT *knocks back yet another drink. The sounds of men cheering and clapping.*

The wheel turns into spinning stars.

SCENE SIX: A JOB OFFER ON THE BEACH

MOTT *staggers drunk towards the beach. The sounds of Broome in the distance. He is in very high spirits.*

KAZUHIKO *is at the water's edge.*

MOTT: Still here!

KAZUHIKO: Haven't left.

MOTT: But your boat has.

KAZUHIKO: You can see it out there.

KAZUHIKO *offers* MOTT *the opera glasses.*

MOTT: In my current condition neither your glasses nor my binoculars would help.

He plonks himself down beside KAZUHIKO. HANIF *and* SAKAMOTO, *also happy gamblers, stagger across the rear of the stage laughing. They take a piss and softly croon melancholy, romantic love songs from their homelands.*

KAZUHIKO: Drunk?

MOTT: Gloriously.

KAZUHIKO: First night of the lay-up.

MOTT: And my first night in Broome.

KAZUHIKO: Whee—the fleet's back! You went whoring, gambling?

MOTT: Guilty. But only to the latter charge. Do you know your father smokes opium?

KAZUHIKO: Yes.

MOTT: Not for the pleasure.

KAZUHIKO: No—for the pain.

Pause. They both look out to sea.

When I was seven he came towards me crawling on his hands and knees—begging for forgiveness.

Soft light on MR TANAKA, *still sitting upstage centre in the black void.*

My mother was dead—an accident in King Sound.

The luminous black pearl from Scene One reappears, floating above MR TANAKA.

He'd been drinking. He knew a patch of shell—where it was. She was strong, and he'd taken her there to bring up pearlshell. But a shark attack—he hadn't counted on that.

In the upstage space, the shark kite sweeps over MR TANAKA *swallowing the pearl. The void turns red then blacks out.*

MOTT: I'm—sorry. If you could have one wish what would it be?

KAZUHIKO: Apart from wishing her back? To escape, from here.

MOTT: To?

KAZUHIKO: Japan—so he can die happily.

MOTT: And then?

KAZUHIKO: Whatever's there would have to be better than what he and I endure at the moment.

MOTT: Endure? That sounds— [*He stands unsteadily.*] Sort of like my cue. I won't beat about the bush—I'm new to Broome, and if tonight's taught me anything, I'll need all the help I can get. What say I hire you?

KAZUHIKO: Me—go to sea?

MOTT: No—on land. In the office—the yard. You know these people— the industry, how it works. You'd liaise with the divers and crews— be on hand when the need, say, for translation arose.

KAZUHIKO: Translation I can handle.

MOTT: Then it's settled? I think you and I could work together well enough, don't you? Good.

KAZUHIKO: What?

MOTT: That your boat's gone out.

KAZUHIKO: Could be it's also come in.

MOTT smiles—a kindly, befuddled drunk.

MOTT: [*shouting*] Life! Who'd be dead, eh?

He starts to leave, but trips and falls.

Ooops—didn't see the banana skin!

MOTT *lays there laughing.*

There is a clap of thunder. MR TANAKA, *who has not moved since losing at cards, sways, then keels over.*

There is the sound of rain mingled with faint traces of a radio news broadcast about the impending war in Europe.

In the background, MR TANAKA, *unable to get up, starts to crawl away on his stomach. He uses his hands and feet like a turtle.*

The light intensifies on KAZUHIKO. *He closes his eyes and tips his face heavenward.* HANIF *and* SAKAMOTO*'s singing starts to sound like frogs croaking in the rain.*

A huge grin breaks out on KAZUHIKO*'s face.*

The sound of frogs croaking builds in the soundtrack. There's the chatter too of a monkey. MOTT *is still on the ground still laughing. The radio sound effects swell.*

Blackout.

The sound becomes harsh—like stones falling on a corrugated iron roof.

SCENE SEVEN: A DAY IN THE YARD

The downstage black gauze disappears, the upstage white curtain tracks on. We are in Anglo-Oriental's shed next morning. We hear the sound of crews chipping away at pearl shells. KAZUHIKO *and* MOTT *enter, talking loudly above the noise.* MOTT *is very hung over.*

KAZUHIKO: The bags of pearlshell are trucked along Streeter Jetty by narrow-gauge rail. Then the raw shell's stacked and sorted according to what lugger and crew it comes from—

They come across two workers (played by the puppeteers) cleaning shells with tomahawks.

WORKER 1: Welcome to Broome, Mr Mott.

MOTT: Morning.

WORKER 2: Welcome to Broome, Mr Mott.

MOTT: Thank you.

WORKER 1: Sore head—drank too much.

WORKER 2: Sore dick—too much jiggy-jig!

MOTT *smiles weakly.*

KAZUHIKO: [*pointing*] That's where the shell's cleaned—the gunk chipped off. The mother of pearl's then graded, weighed, packed and stored, ready for export, in those other sheds there.

MOTT: Ummmnn.

KAZUHIKO: Your father told you none of this?

MOTT: If he did—

KAZUHIKO: You weren't listening—well I wouldn't let too many people know that or it really will be a case of 'Welcome to Broome, Mr Mott'.

MOTT: My problem is I can value a pearl. That's where my expertise lies. But the ins and outs of the button trade, the uses mother of pearl's put to making furniture, cigarette cases, fans, souvenirs, women's combs. What do I know about any of that?

Before KAZUHIKO *can answer:*

Not my only problem however—the shareholders are at me for a report. How seaworthy's the fleet? What would it fetch, were it sold? What state's the equipment in?

KAZUHIKO: Regatta Day'll do a lot of that work for you.

MOTT: Regatta Day?

KAZUHIKO: It ends the first week of the lay-up. Foot races, boat races, a wrestling tournament, and that night, the Broome Bachelors' Ball.

MOTT: Sounds ominous.

KAZUHIKO: I wouldn't know, it's not really for us coloured folk. Thing is, nautically speaking, the big Regatta Day drawcard's a lugger race across Roebuck Bay and back. Fascinating—if you like watching paint dry. But once the harvest's in, come Wednesday or Thursday, everyone you see round here'll be getting their boats in shipshape working order.

MOTT: So?

KAZUHIKO: So no new equipment can be used. Only the gear each lugger had on board during the season. The judges go over every boat with a fine tooth-comb, making all sorts of lists. Start with their paperwork and the kind of report you're after will be well on the way.

MOTT: Good thinking.

KAZUHIKO: Unless I'm mistaken, thinking's what you'll be paying me for. When will you be paying me?

MOTT: When's Regatta Day?

KAZUHIKO: Saturday.

MOTT: How's Saturday sound?

> SAKAMOTO *enters. He grabs* KAZUHIKO *and talks rapidly to him in Japanese.*

KAZUHIKO: What!?

> HANIF *enters, also grabs* KAZUHIKO, *and talks rapidly to him in Malay.*

This I do not believe!

MOTT: Believe what?

> *More talk, including the words 'Tanaka-san'.*

Tanaka-san! Your father! I recognised that bit!

KAZUHIKO: You were there! Why didn't you stop it?! I knew getting a job with you was too good to be true!

> SAKAMOTO *starts dragging* KAZUHIKO *off with him.* HANIF *tries to drag* KAZUHIKO *his way. A tug of war develops.*

MOTT: Will somebody tell me what's happening?!

HANIF: [*in Malay*] Last night.

KAZUHIKO: Last night.

SAKAMOTO: [*in Japanese*] Gambling.

KAZUHIKO: Gambling.

SAKAMOTO: Ah so so! Gambling.

HANIF: Gambling.

SAKAMOTO: [*in Japanese*] He pledged three years of your labour in a bet with me.

KAZUHIKO: [*translating while* SAKAMOTO *is talking*] He pledged three years of my labour?! In a bet with him!

SAKAMOTO: [*in Japanese—pleased*] And lost.

KAZUHIKO: And lost.

HANIF: [*in Malay*] And he pledged three years of your labour in a bet
with me too.

KAZUHIKO: [*translating while* HANIF *is talking*] He pledged three years
of my labour in a bet with him.

HANIF: [*in Malay*] And lost that too.

KAZUHIKO: And lost that too!

> HANIF *and* SAKAMOTO *are shouting again.*

And now they're fighting over the small matter of who gets me
first. I'm a dead man. Six years helping crew their luggers. I'll kill
him. He gambles, he drinks, he smokes, he's hopeless. I'll kill him.
Arggghhh!

> *The workers have long ceased chipping pearlshell and stand
> there, mouths agog.*

> *Then the commotion stops.* MOTT *has produced his pistol.*

MOTT: He—works—for me!

> HANIF *and* SAKAMOTO *are shocked.*

BOTH: But—

MOTT: I hired him.

BOTH: But—

MOTT: Yesterday. And if either of you want to risk a bullet—fine. But I
don't really need this, do I? This is a white country, and I bet white
law takes a very dim view of the bet we're talking about!

> *They think for a moment then, snarling and scowling, exit
> muttering 'Saichi Tanaka-san, kill, death, murder', etc.* MOTT
> *addresses the puppeteers.*

You can get back to work—and you [*to* KAZUHIKO] I suggest you
make for Streeter Jetty to keep those trucks of pearlshell moving.

> *But* KAZUHIKO *doesn't stir.*

I said Streeter Jetty!

> MOTT *exits. Lights focus on* KAZUHIKO.

SCENE EIGHT: TURTLE BEACH

The scene transforms to a stretch of sand. A crackly 1934 recording of 'Whispering' by the Comedy Harmonists. It continues under the scene.

A turtle slowly makes its way across the stage. KAZUHIKO *watches the turtle on its lumbering journey. After a while* SAKAMOTO *and* HANIF *enter running. They're children. They stop when they see the turtle and turn on it. They begin beating it with sticks.* HANIF *and* SAKAMOTO *flip the turtle over on its back. They rain blows down on its underbelly then, laughing, retreat upstage where they stand with their backs to us.*

KAZUHIKO *turns and hastens out.*

Upside down, downstage MR TANAKA*'s head comes out of the turtle 'shell'. Panting. Red-eyed. Alarmed. Blackout.*

SCENE NINE: A BIT OF BUNRAKU

Lights back up. The old man's where he was, on his back—but actually in bed. Two unwanted visitors are about to call by. A thumping is heard.

HANIF *and* SAKAMOTO *turn to address the old man. He scrambles to cover himself better with the sheet that was so recently a turtle shell. Drums and a range of musical effects heighten the menace of the scene.*

As HANIF *and* SAKAMOTO *advance, two operators appear supporting a one third human-size puppet costumed as* TANAKA SENIOR.

SAKAMOTO: If you were a puppet, old man…
HANIF: Consider your fate…
SAKAMOTO: Not a pretty state…
HANIF: To be in.
SAKAMOTO: Pretty soon you'd be missing an arm.
        A puppeteer removes and pockets an arm from the puppet.
HANIF: Missing both arms.
        There goes the other arm.
SAKAMOTO: Missing a leg.
HANIF: Missing both legs.

The puppeteers pluck away the legs. Is this a dream the old guy's having? Or how he views his predicament?

SAKAMOTO: Pretty soon a torso.
HANIF: You'd be—you know…
SAKAMOTO: Nothing—a bundle of pain.
HANIF: Got the nerves and feelings of a human…
SAKAMOTO: And the head—but can't scratch yourself…
HANIF: Can't wave yourself goodbye…
SAKAMOTO: Can't walk or even crawl yourself…
HANIF: Under a rock to die.

> *With what's left of the puppet, the puppeteers have demonstrated this sorry plight. As* HANIF *and* SAKAMOTO *sit alongside* TANAKA SENIOR *the puppeteers retire to the rear to reassemble and recostume the puppet.*

SAKAMOTO: You owe me money, old man!
HANIF: You owe me too!
BOTH: Can pay—can pay?
TANAKA: Cannot.
SAKAMOTO: Then in a spot of bother.
HANIF: Wouldn't you say?
SAKAMOTO: Last night you sign your son's labour away.
HANIF: But today we go for son.
SAKAMOTO: It can't be done.
HANIF: Has old man Saichi Tanaka-san—
SAKAMOTO: Got any thoughts? Got anything to say?
HANIF: About the way things stand?

> *Wrapped mummy-like in the sheet,* TANAKA SENIOR *stands bleary-eyed, hung-over and regretting last night's fun.*

TANAKA: Our fate is indeed a most peculiar thing, is it not?
SAKAMOTO: Agreed.
TANAKA: We generally know what we're coming from—where we've been—what's happened to us—our story so far.
SAKAMOTO: [*softly agreeing*] So so so.
TANAKA: As to where we are located,
    What we've got ourselves into,

The position, this second, this minute, we are in,
That we usually also know with some precision.
HANIF: But where we're headed?
TANAKA: Hmm—there a similar sense of detail, the same certainty, eludes us.
SAKAMOTO: So desu ne.
HANIF: And?
TANAKA: Nothing. It's just—peculiar.

A pause. It's plain the old man's stalling for time. He's been between them, peering over the stage edge as into the abyss. They yank him down to sit with them afresh.

SAKAMOTO: To be frank what we find peculiar's this:
HANIF: I want Kazuhiko to work off your debt!
SAKAMOTO: And I want Kazuhiko to work off your debt!
HANIF: Two people you owe.
SAKAMOTO: But only one son.
HANIF: One son.
SAKAMOTO: But two people to pay.
HANIF: He's not—but were Kazuhiko a puppet—
SAKAMOTO: And were he in a puppet play:

The puppeteers turn back into the action. The puppet they now display is costumed in shirts and shorts like KAZUHIKO. They ceremonially carry it forward. And again musical accompaniment marks this new chapter.

HANIF: Hanif Mohammed Putu Rodrigues da Costa would call for the boy and say:
   'Kazuhiko's three years with me begins today,
   he can start by hauling shell'.
   And I'd haul the boy away.
SAKAMOTO: But in the *genkan* or out in the street
   You'd happen into or otherwise meet—
HANIF: Sakamoto Fuji who'd say—
SAKAMOTO: 'Hold up—how can this be?
   Kazuhiko starts with me today as a deckhand',
   And I'd drag Kazuhiko off.

HANIF: Peculiar, eh? [*Loudly to* TANAKA] Only one son!

SAKAMOTO: [*very loudly in* TANAKA's *ear*] But two people who want him to help crew their luggers!

HANIF: Which bugger gets Kazuhiko first?
Sakamoto—or me?

SAKAMOTO: To be or not to be?

HANIF: What way lies joy?

SAKAMOTO: Do we halve the boy?

> *Behind them the puppeteers have been wresting the puppet first one way, then the other. Now it splits down the middle. They hang their heads and the puppet halves dangle from their hands.*

HANIF: Or is there another way?

SAKAMOTO: Can our old friend foresee
A better end to such a problem puppet play?

> *Pause. The old man mulls this over and then:*

TANAKA: Takarazuka! Yes I can, for:

> *Lights change.* MR TANAKA *leaps to his feet. Big noise, smoke and blinding light as the rear screen parts and into the room steps a beautiful young Japanese woman in traditional costume. She has full make-up and carries a closed fan as if its the hilt of a sword. The heroine in a 'Girl's-own Takarazuka' romance.*

A woman warrior enters the fray!
She beheads, then sends you both to hell!
In love with my son those two lovers they
Gallop away—to China!

> *All of which happens. The sitting* SAKAMOTO *and* HANIF *are suddenly headless*—MISS KITSO *has slain them with her 'sword' and they've drawn their heads into their shirts. The black-clad puppeteers—reforming the halved puppet* KAZUHIKO—*hand it to her. She clasps her lover and mounts a steed (old man* TANAKA*). The tableau 'Riding to China' is triumphantly formed. We hear the old man's voice over:*

TANAKA: [*voice-over, brightly*] Safe and sound in China, Kazuhiko takes the name Takanohana. He becomes a sumo wrestler of note and a

great favourite of Empress Wu. His brave and devoted wife—now
known as Shir-lee—trains an army and defeats the Mongol hordes.
They send for me. I join them—and spend my days winning many
farting competitions in Schezuan—living to be a hundred and three.

*The woman warrior, the puppeteers and the puppet withdraw
back through the screen. But the old man can't escape with these
'figments of his imagining'. He's left alone and turns back to his
tormentors. He stands there, scratching his belly.*

TANAKA: That's how it ends—that puppet play.

He farts. It's the cue for HANIF *and* SAKAMOTO *to poke their
heads back out of their costumes. Old man* TANAKA's *fantasy is
over.*

SAKAMOTO: You're dreaming, old man.

HANIF: And you stink.

SAKAMOTO: As do your deeds.

HANIF: But is he?

SAKAMOTO: Dreaming?

They stand. Hearing a strange eerie music, they narrate:

BOTH: Nothing quite as peculiar took place. But as Saichi Tanaka knelt
between us rueing the fact that he owed us his son's labour—

SAKAMOTO: An event of note did occur—

HANIF: And it did involve a her.

*The screen parts to reveal the same woman. She holds an open
fan in front of her face and steps demurely into the space. She
dances a dance of supplication, gesturing with the fan.*

WOMAN: Please forgive him.

SAKAMOTO: Who—

HANIF: Is—

SAKAMOTO: She?

WOMAN: Forgive him if you can,
   My Uncle is a foolish
   But not a totally wicked man.

She bows her head and spreads the fan across her face. HANIF
and SAKAMOTO *are open-mouthed, staring at the beautiful*

young woman. The old man is equally astonished by what he sees. Freeze: musical flourish.

This tableau holds for a beat. Then HANIF *and* SAKAMOTO *'exit' to either side of the stage. One will be handed flowers. The other a large bottle of sake.*

Meanwhile the old man draws closer to this mysterious and alluring woman who lowers her fan. We hear KAZUHIKO*'s voice or he raises the wig he's donned.*

KAZUHIKO: It's me, dog-brain, trying to save your bacon.

The old man smiles. Then:

TANAKA: Dance.

KAZUHIKO: Dance?

TANAKA: Clap.

KAZUHIKO: Clap?

TANAKA: They're coming back. Wheee!

KAZUHIKO: Wheee!

Music: 'H'lo Baby' recorded in 1930 by Jack Hylton and his Orchestra. To the song HANIF *and* SAKAMOTO *re-enter bearing gifts. They smile at the woman, wave, seek her permission to dance, etc. As they frolic,* TANAKA SENIOR *and* MISS KITSO *sway, clapping hands in encouragement.*

When the song ends the rivals look set to charge each other.

HANIF: Flowers better!

SAKAMOTO: O—sake better!

The old man appeals for decorum.

TANAKA: Gentlemen please.

HANIF: I'll get more flowers.

SAKAMOTO: I'll get more sake.

They exit. TANAKA *and* MISS KITSO *are alone.* KAZUHIKO *removes the wig.*

TANAKA: I thought I pawned your mother's bridal kimono.

KAZUHIKO: Aunt Eki got it back.

TANAKA: Hmm. So what next?

KAZUHIKO: How many steps ahead do you think I am!

He puts the wig on his father.

TANAKA: H'lo baby!

Blackout.

SCENE TEN: THAT NIGHT IN THE YARD

Against a faint radio broadcast about the trouble in Europe, MOTT *is downstage in a shaft of light.*

MOTT: [*to the audience*] I was to first hear the name Miss Kitso working back that evening. A noise in the Anglo-Oriental yard drew me to investigate. What I saw filled me with fear and trepidation.

In the dark we hear HANIF *and* SAKAMOTO.

SAKAMOTO: Closer, my lovely—Mr Granite would like to meet you.

HANIF: Closer yourself, my steel would like to plant the kris of death.

SAKAMOTO: Miss Kitso loves me, she loves you not.

HANIF: To even speak Miss Kitso's name brings you one step closer to your end—you infidel!

SAKAMOTO *holds a large rock above his head.* HANIF *brandishes his kris. The assailants charge, but, because it's dark, miss—or miscalculate—each other's position. The hunt restarts.*

SAKAMOTO: I said closer, you dog.

HANIF: Closer yourself!

MOTT: [*to the audience*] The night was dark but (though rather better than they) I could see how sooner or later these two would locate one another. It was a case of act now or forever hold my peace. With visions of mangled, bleeding bodies swimming before my eyes, I took one pace forward and opening my mouth to protest… fainted.

MOTT *drops to the deck.* SAKAMOTO *and* HANIF *hear the body fall. They wonder what's what.*

SAKAMOTO: Was that you, my little bantam?

HANIF: Have you met your end, you fish ball?

They discover MOTT *'s body.*

SAKAMOTO: Oh no!

HANIF: Did you do that?

SAKAMOTO: It wasn't me!

HANIF: It's not my kris!

> SAKAMOTO *drops his rock dangerously close to the prone* MOTT *whose body reacts galvanically to this event.* HANIF *likewise divests himself of his weapon, bringing a second galvanic flutter from* MOTT *as the kris sticks in the earth beside him.*

SAKAMOTO: Kazuhiko!

HANIF: He'll know what's best.

SAKAMOTO: I'll get him.

HANIF: What? Go to Saichi Tanaka-san's and dally with Miss Kitso? Aw no you don't. You wait here with him and I'll go.

SAKAMOTO: I'll go.

HANIF: I'll go.

SAKAMOTO: I said—

HANIF: I said—

> *They halt their exit. They return to retrieve their weapons and, to a musical sting, prepare to begin a kyogen-style exit in a yet more antagonistic manner—except* MOTT *revives. They pause. And they will smile.*

MOTT: What—now?

SAKAMOTO: In love, Mr Mott.

HANIF: With the same woman.

SAKAMOTO: Been fighting for her.

HANIF: All day—and into the night.

MOTT: You're both covered in blood—

> MOTT *faints afresh. They recommence—to a series of musical stings—their still-fighting exit.*

SAKAMOTO: I'll go.

HANIF: I'll go.

SAKAMOTO: Oh no you won't.

HANIF: Oh yes I will.

SAKAMOTO: I'll go.
HANIF: I'll go!

Blackout.

SCENE ELEVEN: MOTT SEEKS SENSE

The white rear curtain opens to reveal KAZUHIKO *with a tray of glasses and old man* TANAKA *toting a whiskey decanter. They come forward to join* MOTT *who is on his feet but sweating profusely and looking woosey.*

MOTT: Coming to—some time later—in the cosier confines of my home I found not the divers, but Kazuhiko in attendance, saying...
KAZUHIKO: ... and so you see.
MOTT: Problem solved?
KAZUHIKO: Yes.
MOTT: His father—also present—
TANAKA: A very good drop, Mr Mott.
MOTT: Was nearing the end of what must have been—since I'd filled it that morning—a longish battle with my best whiskey decanter. I'm sorry—being in the tropics seems to have got the better of me—I'm afraid you'll have to repeat all you've said.
TANAKA: My niece.
KAZUHIKO: My cousin.
TANAKA: My brother.
MOTT: Bit by bit I try to make sense of what I hear.
KAZUHIKO: My uncle.
TANAKA: In Sydney.
MOTT: A relative of Saichi-san's has died?
TANAKA: Burdened with not just a son to look after—also a niece.
MOTT: There's a Miss Tanaka?
TANAKA: Kitso like a daughter to me now, Mr Mott.
MOTT: And she?
TANAKA: Like you, Mr Mott.
KAZUHIKO: A recent arrival in Broome.
MOTT: How recent?
KAZUHIKO: Today.

MOTT: I see. But I didn't really. And took a whiskey myself, in case in that direction clarity of some kind lay.

TANAKA: It never rains, Mr Mott, but it pours.

The old man pours MOTT *a slug.*

MOTT: It appeared.

TANAKA: Hanif—

KAZUHIKO: And Sakamoto—

MOTT: I wondered when they'd come into it—had, on encountering the girl, become besotted with her charms.

Enter HANIF *and* SAKAMOTO *and the old man pours for them.*

HANIF: In love, Mr Mott.

SAKAMOTO: In love at first sight.

HANIF: Here.

SAKAMOTO: Here.

Each tables for MOTT, *on the drinks tray, a mother's keep.*

MOTT: 'Here' being?

HANIF: Preliminary gifts.

SAKAMOTO: For Miss Kitso.

TANAKA: Part of bride price, Mr Mott.

MOTT: Bride price?

TANAKA: As we say in Japan—all's well that ends well.

MOTT: I can't pretend to know how this will end but I do begin to see what's proposed. These two have waived their right to your labour in exchange for a chance to marry the girl?

KAZUHIKO: Correct.

MOTT: And your father would like their gifts valued to help him decide who the most suitable suitor is?

KAZUHIKO: So so.

MOTT: And if the price is right.

TANAKA: Back to Taiji!

KAZUHIKO: Escape, Mr Mott.

MOTT: You're off the hook—but your cousin is on it! And that worries nobody here a jot!

KAZUHIKO: Why would it?

MOTT: The buying and selling of brides!

TANAKA: This Asian way, Mr Mott.

MOTT: [*to the audience*] Suddenly the gap between how I and these people thought felt as wide as the Yangtze. And the room, even as its fan circled overhead, seemed as close as the hand with which I wiped my sweating—almost feverish—brow. I'm sorry. I don't think I can do justice to all this right now.

Again MOTT *hits the deck. This time in slow motion, accompanied by slurred sound effects. The shadow of the fan swirls overhead.*

HANIF: He very good at falling over, that man.

TANAKA: Like father like son. Old Mr Mott the same. See blood, see a problem, down he'd go.

SAKAMOTO: You think it the whiskey white people drink?

They consider this. TANAKA SENIOR, HANIF *and* SAKAMOTO *drain their glasses. They fall down. Left standing, holding decanter and tray,* KAZUHIKO *isn't amused.*

KAZUHIKO: Maybe this time we really should fetch the doctor.

Still laughing, they get up. But perhaps MOTT*'s fainting problems should be treated rather more seriously.*

Blackout.

SCENE TWELVE: MOTT'S DELIRIUM

The sound of radio reports of war in Europe grows.

The stage is filled with Mott family photographs.

HANIF, SAKAMOTO *and* MR TANAKA *begin to drag* MOTT *upstage.*

The soundtrack builds with sounds of fire crackling. It is as if MOTT *is being dragged to his death.*

A huge Star of David appears in the void.

Flames spring up in the black void.

MOTT *is hurled into the flames.*

The images of the photos crack and burn.

Blackout. Cut to:

SCENE THIRTEEN: A NEW LOVE BLOOMS

The beach. Some days have passed. The sound of waves. MOTT *and* MR TANAKA *meet.* MOTT *looks terrible.*

TANAKA: [*bowing*] Mr Mott.
MOTT: [*bowing uneasily*] Mr Tanaka.
TANAKA: You very sick man my son tells me.
MOTT: On the mend, on the mend.

> MOTT *produces the drawstring bags he got some nights ago and proffers them to* TANAKA SENIOR.

I return these—worth a tidy sum I must say—you'll find my written valuations inside.
TANAKA: Please, keep them.

> MR TANAKA *offers him another little bag.*

And this.

> *He gives* MOTT *another bag.*

And this.
MOTT: More gifts?
TANAKA: Those two are still trying to influence my decision.
MOTT: You'd like them valued as well?
TANAKA: If you would be so kind. And this.

> *He hands him a scroll.*

The proposed marriage contract between Sakamoto and Miss Kitso.

> *He hands him an envelope.*

And this.

> MOTT *smells it—it's obviously perfumed.*

Marriage contract—Miss Kitso and Hanif. They'd like you to keep everything until decision is made.
MOTT: Me?

TANAKA: Sort of thing father would have done.

MOTT: [*reading*] My name's down here.

TANAKA: As a witness, Miss Kitso's idea.

MOTT: Again the sort of thing my father would have done?

> MR TANAKA *smiles and nods.*

They lease my family's luggers, and supply Anglo-Oriental with pearlshell. I get the message. I must say I feel a tad queer the guardian of so much booty.

TANAKA: You white man, Mr Mott. In Broome—safe as a safe.

> MR TANAKA *sees someone coming.*

[*Whispering*] Shh… There she is.

MOTT: Who?

TANAKA: Miss Kitso—with Hanif.

MOTT: So finally I get to see the woman all this fuss is about.

> *Music: 'So Rare' (1937 recording by Hildegarde with Orchestra).*

> MISS KITSO *appears as if gliding, upstage. Cherry blossoms fall from the sky and the puppeteers scatter cherry blossoms over her as she walks.*

> HANIF *enters. He is dressed to the nines in his best clothes. He has come to court* MISS KITSO. *She keeps ignoring him. When this is no longer possible, she slaps him with her fan. He smiles— holding his cheek. She smiles.*

> *From their vantage point,* MOTT *and the old man see all this.*

She's giving him something.

TANAKA: A small gift.

MOTT: A ribbon.

> *She ceremonially bestows on* HANIF *a brightly-coloured ribbon He exits with it held to his heart.* MISS KITSO *stays.*

TANAKA: They make good couple, yes?

MOTT: She's certainly a fine-looking creature.

TANAKA: In both Wakayama and Sydney her mother was considered a great beauty, Japanese-style. It shows, don't you think—in the daughter…?

She bends to look at her footwear. MOTT *is mesmerised.*

You like her new zori, Mr Mott?

MOTT: Zori?

TANAKA: Japanese sandals. Kazuhiko bought them for Kitso at Yasukichi Murakami's Nishioka store. On the promise of the wages he'll get from you.

MOTT: He'll get those—not a worry in the world.

TANAKA: In Japan a woman's feet are thought an attractive part of the body. Exotic—or do I mean—?

MOTT: Erotic perhaps?

Enter SAKAMOTO. *He too is dressed in his Sunday best.*

TANAKA: Also make good couple, yes?

MOTT—*fascinated by the courtship rituals—doesn't reply.*

SAKAMOTO *will also receive a ribbon but of a different colour. And exit happily clutching this precious item.*

Not easy, Mr Mott, deciding. Must weigh up what each man has to offer, judge their character, their prospects. And take into account girl's wishes.

MOTT: You'll be doing that?

TANAKA: My motto. A little bit eastern way—a little bit west—is best. Yes?

MOTT: I'm relieved she'll have some say.

The song finishes.

TANAKA: Must join niece, Mr Mott.

MOTT: Of course.

The old man moves to MISS KITSO. *She listens to him, then looks back towards* MOTT. *As for* MOTT, *it's like the colour's returned to his cheeks.*

[*To the audience*] From top to toe a vision of Eastern perfection. The girl's hair—with its mother of pearl combs—were it let down how many men I wondered would drown in it like carp in a net.

MR TANAKA *is ushering* MISS KITSO *towards* MOTT.

Seconds later two of the most delicately-shaped feet I've ever seen have entered my field of vision.

MR TANAKA *and his niece arrive.* MOTT'*s eyeline moves slowly up her body from her feet to her fan-covered face.*

TANAKA: My unworthy niece, Mr Mott, Miss Kitso Tanaka.

MISS KITSO *bows, smiles, and keeps her head low.*

MOTT: I'm honoured.

MISS KITSO *says nothing.*

TANAKA: Niece very shy.

MOTT: How much say can someone so shy have?

MISS KITSO *puts her fan across her mouth.*

TANAKA: Will be at Saturday's sumo, Mr Mott? I referee. In Broome, Saichi Tanaka still Number One—in some things.

MOTT *is not sure what to say but asks:*

MOTT: Will Miss Kitso be attending?

MISS KITSO *shakes her head, eyes cast down.*

TANAKA: Niece unable to. Me, too busy refereeing. Kazuhiko? Regatta Day! Eiaa! That's the Broome he hates! No other chaperone I can trust.

MOTT: I'd gladly accompany Miss Kitso to the sumo if that's a help.

TANAKA: Honto-ni? Good to know niece will be in safe hands.

The old man manages a deep bow. MOTT *bows back.*

Will make big decision after wrestling!

KITSO *bows less deeply and the two exit, going backwards upstage bowing and bowing and bowing.*

They exit gliding from view. MOTT'*s alone.*

Music starts. A 1937 recording of Fred Astaire singing 'Things Are Looking Up'.

MOTT *turns to the audience—a spotlight claims him as verse one is heard.*

At the start of verse two, he runs upstage to catch a last glimpse of MISS KITSO.

He begins to sing and dance like Fred Astaire. As the song continues the space fills with projections of flowers.

Still in their finery HANIF *and* SAKAMOTO *enter and during a dance break a golden sun rises inside the void.*

The routine builds to a big finish.

At its end everything returns to everyday reality, with MOTT *alone.* KAZUHIKO *enters on his way somewhere.*

MOTT: Oi! Kazuhiko! [MOTT *crosses to him.*] I've not been up to much this week, have I?

KAZUHIKO: Where would you be without me?

MOTT: Where would I be without you? All's well at the yard?

KAZUHIKO: Harvest's in, cleaning, sorting, grading's almost complete.

MOTT: Anything else I've missed?

KAZUHIKO: Nothing of note, bar Hanif and Sakamoto's rivalry for my cousin's hand. It's spread to their crews. All jailed last night for fighting. The whole of Broome's saying the sooner that girl's married off the better.

    KAZUHIKO *goes to leave.* MOTT *detains him.*

MOTT: And she?

KAZUHIKO: What?

MOTT: What's she—how's she, herself, taking it?

KAZUHIKO: Put it this way: if I were her I'd be flattered by the attention—glad of the gifts—and close to overwhelmed by the whole situation.

MOTT: Give her my regards.

KAZUHIKO: Your…?

MOTT: My regards. Tell her I'm thinking about her.

    He exits, humming the love song we've heard. KAZUHIKO *is puzzled. The old man enters to him.*

TANAKA: What did Mr Mott have to say?

KAZUHIKO: Must be the fever still—wants me to give Miss Kitso his regards.

TANAKA: That shouldn't be too hard, should it?

KAZUHIKO: Ha ha!

> KAZUHIKO *exits. Left behind, the old man gives the audience a truly wicked grin.*

> *Loud drumming. Blackout.*

SCENE FOURTEEN: THE SUMO. DAY OF THE BIG CUSHIONS

The drummers enter, followed by a large (four-person) Chinese dragon with a giant pearl in its mouth. It performs a spectacular dance accompanied by the sound of firecrackers exploding.

At the end of the dance the dragon exits, but the drummers remain on stage. They settle into position as the roof above the sumo ring flies in upstage above the black void.

MR TANAKA *enters in the costume of a sumo referee, leading* MOTT *and* MISS KITSO. *He sees them settled down then goes back to check preparations for the sumo.*

MOTT *is trying to make sense of his sumo program.*

MOTT: And this is who?

KITSO: Shikishima. East.

MOTT: Versus?

KITSO: Tamakasuga.

MOTT: West.

KITSO: Mahjong has the four winds—sumo the two directions. East and West. Higashi to nishi.

MOTT: So Shikishima and Tamakasuga fight each other in?

KITSO: Round two—bout four.

MOTT: How many bouts per round?

KITSO: It varies, but in round two? Sixteen.

MOTT: Then?

KITSO: Round three—eight bouts. Then the quarter final. Four.

MOTT: The semi-final two?

KITSO: So.
MOTT: Until finally—
KITSO: The final.
MOTT: This is going to take a while, isn't it?
KITSO: Sashimi, Mr Mott?
MOTT: I can see why you brought supplies.

To drumming, the first sumo match begins. The puppeteers have been performing the preliminary rituals of the sumo—salt throwing, etc. Now they fight—manipulating cushions that have brightly-painted faces on them to represent the wrestlers.

There will be a series of bouts each with increasingly larger cushions.

As bout one ends, armed with chopsticks, MISS KITSO *is delicately feeding* MOTT *a morsel from her bento box.*

KITSO: You'll partake of some sake, I expect?
MOTT: What—Oh—ha—please.
KITSO: I pour for you. And now—Japanese style—you must pour for me.
MOTT: Really?
KITSO: To pour for oneself in Japan is to be considered a drunk.
MOTT: Is that so?
KITSO: So. Unless your boss or your father is pouring for himself, or your husband, your uncle, your elder brother and so on. In Japan so many exceptions.
MOTT: Does your uncle pour for himself?
KITSO: Of course.
MOTT: He's an exception?
KITSO: No. A drunk.

MOTT *laughs. She giggles into her hand.*

MOTT: [*aside*] The woman even had a sense of humour!

They clink sake cups.

KITSO: Kampai!
MOTT: Kampai!

There is a commotion upstage. At the rear, in sumo outfits, HANIF
and SAKAMOTO *enter from different directions. They meet in
the middle and scowl at each other. They are both worse for
wear. After a week of fighting they have black eyes and wear
bandages, etc.*

TANAKA: Sakamoto Fuji-san!

The crowd cheers.

Hanif Mohammed Putu Rodrigues da Costa!

More cheering.

HANIF *and* SAKAMOTO *acknowledge their supporters. The
second puppeteer and old man* TANAKA *massage them. The
other puppeteer is sweeping the sumo ring.*

Must guard against a repeat of the unfortunate events of 1937. Must
foster good communal relations.

HANIF: Why look at me—I'm no Koepanger. From Sarawak—one
sixth Dyak wrestler, remember?

TANAKA: Cannot forget.

HANIF: And he'll see how well I can wrestle, even Japanese-style.

TANAKA: Cannot forget how you two were at each other's throats in
1937—and have been all week.

SAKAMOTO: What are you saying, old man?

TANAKA: The Koepangers the Macassans the Malays the Filipinos—
they look up to you.

HANIF: And the Japanese?

TANAKA: They look up to him.

VOICES: Sakamoto Fuji-san!

OTHERS: Hanif Hanif Hanif!

HANIF *and* SAKAMOTO *again acknowledge their supporters.*

TANAKA: If you two stay within the rules—if you big men keep the
peace—others will also. Why give the white people an excuse to
make life harder for us?

SAKAMOTO: Bah.

HANIF: Bah.

SAKAMOTO: Ar—

HANIF: Ar—
BOTH: Miss Kitso!

> *They wave in her direction. She is training the opera glasses on them. She waves back. They finger and show off the coloured ribbons she gave them which now trail from their sumo outfits. She passes the opera glasses to* MOTT *who likewise views the wrestlers.*

MOTT: Well well—has someone been giving them ribbons?
KITSO: Has someone been watching me more closely than I thought?
TANAKA: [*calling out*] Top fun, eh Mr Mott?
MOTT: Yes top fun, top fun. Top fun all right, except everything I see and hear around me seems all wrong! Is a pro-slavery petition doing the rounds? Hand me a pen. Where do I sign?
KITSO: You mean this marriage business?
MOTT: What else?
KITSO: You don't approve?
MOTT: Do you really feel comfortable being bid for in this way?
KITSO: Tradition.
MOTT: Tradition.
KITSO: What can we do?
MOTT: Can we go for a walk—I'd like, since your uncle has made me such an interested party—to at least learn your true feelings in the matter. Frankly, the thought of you going to either of those oafs does not fill me with confidence that all is well with the world.
KITSO: Was it ever?
MOTT: Oh? A philosopher even?

> *She bows her head.*

SCENE FIFTEEN: HIGH WINDS IN THE WINGS

To music MOTT *and* KITSO *walk across the stage. As they do, part of a large boab tree slides out from the wall.*

KITSO: Such a beautiful tree.
MOTT: The boab?
KITSO: Planted 1898—by a policeman to mark the birth of his son.

The son perished in the great war—the policeman himself died in 1920—but the boab soldiers on.

MOTT: How do you know about the tree?

He will spread his jacket for her to sit on.

KITSO: My cousin, Mr Mott, knows much about this town.

MOTT: You and he—

KITSO: We talk a lot.

MOTT: You talk far more than I supposed.

KITSO: Is that me—or the sake talking?

MOTT: Here's far enough away from the madding crowd. I'll not detain you for long but I feel obliged to acquaint you with, as it were, the lay of the land.

She seats herself demurely. He remains standing for the moment, a hand on the tree.

In the right inside pocket of my jacket you'll find what's colourfully termed a mother's keep—two of them in fact—each fashioned, I'm told, from the scrotum of a bullock, a drawstring attached. Hanif's offering to your uncle.

KITSO: This pocket?

KITSO *reaches into the suggested jacket pocket.*

MOTT: Yes. Fifteen quite notable pearls, two of them outstanding specimens. One, the Chinese call 'silver-clouded-moon'.

MOTT *picks a pearl from the bag she holds out.*

KITSO: Type of pearl?

MOTT: Type of pearl. The other they term 'starlight-on-a-frosty-night'. [*He rummages in the bag.*] Quite the best example of its kind I've ever set eyes on. Get just these two pearls to the Singapore market, to Tokyo, Shanghai, New York, and your uncle will be four, perhaps five, even six hundred pounds richer.

KITSO: Eyes wide with surprise, Mr Mott?

MOTT: [*looking at her*] And what eyes they are?

KITSO: Pearls so small but worth so much? I should marry Hanif?

MOTT: Should you?

He returns the two pearls to their bag.

KITSO: You think Sakamoto the wiser choice?

MOTT: Let's hear from him, shall we? [*He kneels to pull out another bag.*] This time from my left inside pocket, another mother's keep, again, an assortment of pearls, again worth a great deal, and with them this fine-tooled leather wallet containing a wad of cash. A thousand pounds in all—no need to count it, I already have—in all likelihood the man's life savings. It comes with what I take to be a poem.

> MOTT *unrolls a little scroll and* KITSO *reads the Japanese characters.*

KITSO: 'For as long as the cherry blossoms bloom and fall, for as long as the sea rises, and the winds play their music, for as long as the mountains stand, for that long I shall love, cherish, adore and otherwise support Kitso Tanaka—A number one poem from Diver Number One'.

> *He slowly stands, staring down at her, taken by her beauty.*

So Sakamoto is winner, Mr Mott?

MOTT: Does it end there? In my trouser pocket you'll find a lump.

KITSO: The geisha game of surprise surprise!

> *She stands to slip a hand in his trouser pocket.*

A ball?

MOTT: A pearl.

> *She fishes a black pearl from his pocket.*

KITSO: But it's black.

> *Drums rumble. The black gauze rushes across the stage effectively dividing the stage in two. Music plays softly. On the gauze we again see the face of the beautiful young Aboriginal woman. The soundscape now includes the heavily amplified sound of her breath.*

I've never seen such a thing.

MOTT: Few people have, yet that black pearl is by itself the equal of Sakamoto and Hanif's pearls put together! But don't think of it in isolation—my other pocket, if you will.

> MISS KITSO *reaches into* MOTT'*s other trouser pocket. She pulls out a string of pearls. The music grows louder. A dream-like quality is developing.*

KITSO: This black—these white.

MOTT: As white as your beautiful face.

> *He touches the black pearl she holds so their fingers touch.*

Think of this in combination with that string of white pearls, some twenty-three in number, grade A lustre, of a size and shape attained nowhere but in these waters. In fact arrange them if you will, but with that black beauty at their centre.

> MISS KITSO *kneels and on the spread jacket begins to arrange the pearls in a circle. The music builds under.*

Not enough, sadly, for a whole necklace, but maybe this season, maybe next, three more pearls that shape, size and lustre will come to light and I'll be able to complete what's been the project of several lifetimes. Begun by my grandfather when that black Tahitian wonder came his way, it became my father's dream to complete the string before he died. He didn't manage to do so, but on his death-bed made me vow to make the Mott Family vision of such a necklace a reality.

> *She is looking at the pearls. He is looking at her.*

Does it not take your breath away Miss Kitso, because, as a pearl trader, it fair swallows mine. Whenever I see that circle of pearls I think how beautiful the world can be.

KITSO: And I—?

MOTT: You?

KITSO: Am reminded only of the sumo ring where we should be.

> *Drumming. Cut to the sumo. A strong breeze is slowly building.*

> HANIF *and* SAKAMOTO *are going through the rituals of the sumo—throwing salt, etc. But also looking into the crowd.*

HANIF: Where is she?

TANAKA: Who?

SAKAMOTO: Miss Kitso—numbskull!

TANAKA: She's in the crowd with Mr Mott.

The trio look out into the crowd and are gone.

Cut back to MISS KITSO *and* MOTT. *She speaks as one in a dream.*

KITSO: Here, in fold of obi, I have a small gift from Kazuhiko.

She takes a misshapen piece of baroque pearl from her obi and shows it to MOTT.

A 'double-something', yes?

MOTT: A 'double-button stringer' we term it in the trade.

He takes it and examines it.

KITSO: A bit like me, pretty, but flawed.

MOTT: Don't say that.

He examines the pearl more closely.

KITSO: What if, for a joke, the black pearl necklace had my unworthy bauble behind, like so?

She puts a hand to the back of her neck.

MOTT: Add a double-button stringer! Finish it off with two half pearls, two low-grade but not unattractive blister pearls?

KITSO: With it necklace is a necklace, desu ne?

MOTT: So desu ne!

He kneels to do what she suggests and the result excites him.

You're brilliant! And I'm stunned. In my grandfather's time, in Russia the Czarina would have parted with half Moscow to get her mits on something as perfect!

They stand there struck by the wonder of all this.

MISS KITSO *indicates the treasure his jacket holds.*

KITSO: Hanif this pocket. Sakamoto that. But here?

MOTT: A delicate issue, one I'll approach from two directions, if I may.

KITSO: The East and the West?

MOTT: Higashi to nishi.

MOTT, *in animated fashion, paces, constructing an argument.*

Three grand houses to our right stands whose residence, Miss Kitso? That of Ancel Gregory, pearling master, Town Councillor, pastoralist. A big man in Broome, big as in a success, but big also in that he treats all he meets on their merits irrespective of race, colour or creed. You may have already heard how his best friend is—

KITSO: Yasukichi Murakami.

MOTT: Yasukichi Murakami. Merchant, photographer, inventor, also a big man.

KITSO: Owner of the Nishioka Emporium.

MOTT: And Gregory's long-term partner in many a joint and lucrative venture. Inseparable.

KITSO: Gregory's shadow they call him.

MOTT: You know that story too?

KITSO: Kazuhiko again.

MOTT: You two must talk a great deal.

KITSO: We do.

MOTT: But has he told you how in 1912, when Gregory went back to Europe for a year, he gave Murakami the run of his house? An Oriental, in a whiteman's hacienda, and not doing the cooking! My my—didn't that put noses out of joint, so much so that some call Gregory the—

KITSO: Jap-lover.

MOTT: For a Jew, Miss Kitso, Jap-lover is a term I won't have much trouble living with.

KITSO: Are you saying—?

MOTT: I'm saying that like Ancel Gregory before me I expect to become a very, very good friend of the Japanese community in Broome. [*He looks at her with yearning.*] Yes. Kazuhiko—gambled away in a card game. That I could not accept.

KITSO: Nor could he.

MOTT: And you—subject to the marriage trade! All I could think at first was the poor, poor girl.

KITSO: Poor, I am.

MOTT: And yet how hypocritical was I being? Do not brides come with a dowry attached in most societies? With us Jews for example, match-making remains the rule rather than the exception. Don't I, like you, face the prospect of marriage to a woman chosen for me the minute I return to London?

KITSO: Really?

MOTT: Really.

KITSO: And do you—?

MOTT: Love the woman? Someone I've seen once, and then across a crowded barmitzvah! The idea's an outrage but what can people in our shoes do? Faced with an arranged marriage, do we rebel? Ignore our parents? Flee? And if we escape, where do we escape to?

KITSO: A brave new world.

MOTT: Somewhere our rights, our feelings in matters of the heart will be respected?

KITSO: I sometimes imagine there exists such a place.

MOTT: There ought to—so why not go there? We're young, brave, modern in our thinking—to hell with what our parents and guardians want for us!

KITSO: Could life be that simple?

MOTT: Can't it?

KITSO: Can it?

MOTT: I think it can! But if eloping's not to your liking, Miss Kitso, that necklace there is saying, in the marriage stakes, my hat is in the ring!

The look on MISS KITSO*'s face as she turns away suggests how troubling she finds this unexpected development.*

Unable to restrain himself any further, MOTT *turns her his way and seeks to kiss her. She resists. Then doesn't. Music underscores their passion. They hold the kiss.*

Back at the sumo, HANIF *and* SAKAMOTO *start forward with old man* TANAKA *in tow.*

SAKAMOTO: She's nowhere to be seen!

HANIF: And nor is he!

They turn on MR TANAKA.

TANAKA: Well, how do I know where they've got to?

HANIF: She should be here to see her future husband take the puff out of this adder!

SAKAMOTO: Future husband—you? Not when she learns what squashed flea-meat you've become!

Drums rumble and the old man leads them back to the ring.

MOTT *ends the kiss and gazes into* KITSO*'s eyes.*

MOTT: Am I giddy with love or what—The barnacles of the boats like my own limbs, tremble. The ground beneath me seems to move!

Long pause. But then the penny drops.

[*Softly*] Kazuhiko?

Pause. KAZUHIKO *turns away.*

MOTT *is dumbfounded.* KAZUHIKO *nods yes.*

Music: 'The Moon Got In My Eyes'. A 1937 recording by Hildegarde. The song 'favours' MOTT.

During verse one, KAZUHIKO *begins to slowly take off his disguise.*

KAZUHIKO *has now shed and set down the obi kimono and wig. By the time of the final verse he is standing in his underwear.*

The song finishes. MOTT *faints.* KAZUHIKO *kneels down to bring him around.*

But, but—why?

KAZUHIKO: I've been reared to be a good Japanese son. We thought we'd take those two oafs for all they're worth and get Dad home to Taiji—to die.

MOTT *is silent. They are both embarrassed.*

[*Standing*] Well, come on! Let's do what you said—let's strike out for some brave new world!

MOTT: You can't mean that?

MOTT *stands. We are not sure what he is going to do.*

Long silence.

KAZUHIKO: No. [*Pause.*] No, of course not. Because as usual, the world is pressing in and for this cockroach, this piece of insect life, there is no escape. I'm trapped, aren't I?

SCENE SIXTEEN: KAZUHIKO'S NIGHTMARE, MOTT'S MEMOIR

Loud drumming and a primal scream from KAZUHIKO.

It's a bleak cry of despair—as fearsome as a panic attack—a deep angst that twists and contorts his body.

Projections all over the set make it feel as if KAZUHIKO *is trapped in a net.*

The shark kite again sweeps in upstage.

Drumming builds very loud.

The void goes red.

To a sonic representation of silence, the face of his mother appears again on the black gauze.

Everything freezes. Except for MOTT.

MOTT: Here, with both the moment of my greatest happiness and bitterest disappointment inextricably intertwined, I interrupt my memoir to intrude a meteorological footnote.

> MOTT *begins to range through the space. In effect he'll dance up the weather. The whole cast, except for* KAZUHIKO, *will group behind the gauze looking out.*

MOTT [*voice-over*]: At the onset of any monsoon season cyclones, and their less destructive cousins, typhoons, were (and still are) common on the North-West Australian coast. Coming in from the sea they owe their fearsome strength to that ocean's complex currents. But a less well-publicised phenomenon, known locally as a cockeyed bob, has different and gentler origins. Not to the West, and out to sea, but in the East, the beginnings of a cockeyed bob, with a front seldom more than a mile or two wide, will move across the dry inland. And slowly drift towards the coast. Typically maintaining a mild, almost balmy disposition, such a mere breeze might range the coast, popping in and out of bays and inlets in a corkscrew manner, occasionally a danger to the pearling and fishing fleets, but by and large a harmless avoidable affair. There are times, however, when those small, dry, hot winds will, on meeting the ocean, shrink, contract, buckle in on themselves, and from being so suddenly cooled, acquire the turbulence and fury of a fireball. Then, weaving a crazed path, if such a wind doubles-back inland it can mean dire consequences for all and any settlements in its way. That day in November 1939 one such small desert wind had reached the coast. By dusk it had become what Broome would later term the cockeyed bob to beat all cockeyed bobs!

On the gauze the young woman takes a deep breath in, fills her cheeks with air. The cast are sucked back to their sumo location. The young woman blows out and:

SCENE SEVENTEEN: IT'S AN ILL WIND—OR IS IT?

On stage, the cockeyed bob hits with ferocious force.

The town is blown apart. The roof of the sumo ring blows away.

The black gauze tracks off, but the image of the woman remains projected over the whole space.

The tree trembles then disappears.

At the tournament HANIF *and* SAKAMOTO *are grunting, locked in a sumo embrace. They slowly get blown apart and thrust offstage by the force of the wind.*

In like fashion, 'the lovers' too are flung offstage but not before KAZUHIKO *has bent to pick up Mott's jacket in what seems a casual rather than premeditated attempt to clothe his near nakedness. With him (ta da) goes the loot.*

TANAKA: Fight on, fight on!

Still trying to referee, the old man is lifted off his feet. He clings to the wall, his body horizontal.

What's wrong with you people?! I lived through the cyclones of 1908, 1912, 1913. Compared to them this is nothing!

Debris continues to fly past.

And take the big blow of 1935. Now that really was weather! This! A bit of wind.

The sleeves of his referee's outfit are wrenched from him.

Yes, yes, it's a little like '35! The roof of the Muramatz store went then—

A piece of roof flies past.

And it's gone again—

The kimono rises from where KAZUHIKO *had left it, flying through the air towards him.*

But you can't top 1910 for really bad—!

The kimono wraps itself around him effectively gagging him. He slumps to the ground. Not just the kimono, also Miss Kitso's wig recostumes the old boy.

HANIF *enters against the wind. He calls to* MOTT.

HANIF: Where is she?!

MOTT: Who?

HANIF: Miss Kitso! I must save Miss Kitso...o...o...o...!

Exit HANIF—*blown away.* SAKAMOTO *enters.*

SAKAMOTO: Have you seen her?!

MOTT: Miss Kitso?

SAKAMOTO: Yes—I must save Miss Kitso!

They come and go until the wind stops, suddenly causing them to all fall down.

MOTT: Would Kazuhiko be the Miss Kitso you're after?

He triumphantly pulls the kimono off MR TANAKA.

HANIF: Saichi!?

SAKAMOTO: Tanaka-san!

TANAKA: No! No! Only an old turtle, looking to return to the sea to die!

MOTT: Good idea, you old scum bag! The sea's that way!

MOTT *has gestured towards the audience but the old man rolls over and, turtle-like, starts crawling towards the rear.*

HANIF and SAKAMOTO *are left holding the wig and kimono.*

HANIF: Miss Kitso—the old man?

SAKAMOTO: Cannot be.

HANIF: Cannot.

SAKAMOTO: So often—them together.

HANIF: Miss Kitso—Saichi?

SAKAMOTO: Saichi—Miss Kitso?

MOTT: But who ever saw Kazuhiko with them?

HANIF: Miss Kitso—

SAKAMOTO: Kazuhiko?

HANIF: Kazuhiko—

SAKAMOTO: Miss Kitso?

HANIF: That woman bloody boy all the time?

> *A shocked pause. Then* HANIF *starts to laugh.*

Ha ha. Good joke!

> SAKAMOTO *joins in.*

SAKAMOTO: Top fun!

> *The divers laugh.* MOTT *smiles wanly. They whack him warmly
> on the back. The centre of the cockeyed bob's fury is well and
> truly elsewhere now.*

HANIF: Funny! But lucky!

SAKAMOTO: Lucky! But funny!

MOTT: Why, because you're still alive?

SAKAMOTO: Funny because funny.

HANIF: Lucky because Mr Mott still has our pearls!

SAKAMOTO: And my money!

MOTT: That I do, in my—Ahh, no! My jacket!

> *They hear the sound of an aeroplane starting up.*

The night mail wouldn't take off in this weather, would it?

HANIF: This blow just about over.

MOTT: Then an even bigger blow awaits us all!

> *The plane sound effect builds.* MOTT, HANIF *and* SAKAMOTO *run
> on the spot, headed for the airport.* MOTT *takes out the revolver
> from his pocket, waving it in the air.*

Propellers whirring, the shadow of the plane passes over them.
MOTT *fires into the air after it.*

HANIF *and* SAKAMOTO *swear and collapse in a heap, panting.*
MOTT *stands and watches the plane go. The gun hangs limply in
his hand.*

Bugger!

HANIF *and* SAKAMOTO *are laughing at* MOTT.

Bugger! Bugger! Bugger!

Even MOTT *sees the joke and smiles wryly.*

SCENE EIGHTEEN: PAR AVION

Ambient plane sound effects fade in.

KAZUHIKO, *bare-chested and wearing* MOTT*'s jacket, sits on a mailbag
upstage in the black void. Lit by low cabin light, he is threading the
pearl necklace to fix the black pearl in its centre.*

KAZUHIKO: Broome to Wyndham to Darwin by plane—then the cattle
boat to the Philippines. Purpose of visit? To visit relatives. How
many relatives we got in the Philippines?

The old man's head appears.

TANAKA: Plenty. Tanakas from Taiji there. Tanakas from Taiji in
Hawaii. In Brazil, Peru, California. We everywhere!

KAZUHIKO: How do I look?

He dons the necklace.

TANAKA: If you were a girl—I'd sell you! In fact, in the Philippines I
may have to! Oooo!

KAZUHIKO: What now?

TANAKA: Never seasick, not once.

KAZUHIKO: But airsick?

The old guy spews.

You are disgusting.

TANAKA: I'm evil.

JOHN ROMERIL

A spot favours him as he smiles a wicked triumphant grin.

Their tableau fades.

SCENE NINETEEN: A CODA

Music: 1942 recording by Leslie Hutchinson of 'Take the World Exactly As You Find It'.

MOTT *enters, costumed to suggest it's some years hence and he's in colder climes. The song grows louder.*

At a certain point the turtle enters and makes its way across the stage on its way to the sea. We notice KAZUHIKO *watching, also recostumed. In effect the moment of his father's death is being played out.*

During the music break, a frog and a monkey cross the back of the stage: HANIF *and* SAKAMOTO *play a childhood game.*

MOTT *is on the other side of the stage to* KAZUHIKO. *They look across at each other for a moment. The light intensifies on them.*

MOTT: Back in London I did save my closest relatives from Hitler's clutches. No thanks to you—your theft made it hard.

KAZUHIKO: Thanks to my theft I saved a relative of mine—for a time.

The turtle has disappeared.

MOTT: Otherwise—how goes it?

KAZUHIKO: In the Philippines? You know—wars—you win some, you lose some. An Aboriginal of Japanese extraction, in occupied Manila? I survive.

They turn out front, close their eyes and tip their faces heavenward. As the song continues, a thousand pearls begin to fall from the sky.

Blackout as the song finishes.

Big drumming brings on the curtain calls.

THE END